CW00408862

Happy Beans

Plant-based recipes

For my dad,
Skyrme Lewis
(22/2/1927–9/3/2018),
who never forgot that he loved me.

Happy Beans: Plant-based recipes
Published in Great Britain in 2020 by Graffeg
Limited.

Written by Jane Reynolds copyright © 2020.
Food photography by Huw Jones
copyright © 2020.
Post-production by Matt Braham.
Designed and produced by Graffeg Limited
copyright © 2020.

Graffeg Limited, 24 Stradey Park Business
Centre, Mwrwg Road, Llangennech, Llanelli,
Carmarthenshire, SA14 8YP, Wales, UK.
Tel: 01554 824000. www.graffeg.com.

Jane Reynolds is hereby identified as the author
of this work in accordance with section 77 of the
Copyrights, Designs and Patents Act 1988.

A CIP Catalogue record for this book is available
from the British Library.

ISBN 9781913134273

1 2 3 4 5 6 7 8 9

Happy Beans

Plant-based recipes

Jane Reynolds & Huw Jones

GRAFFEG

Contents

Starters & Sides

1. Gollops (Courgette Fritters)   12

2. Ajvar   16

3. Dolmades   18

4. Taralli Pugilese   22

5. Tempura Okra with Sweet Chilli Dipping Sauce   24

6. Nettle Soup with Beetroot & Walnut Bread   28

7. Peanut Butter, Jalapeño & Gin Jam Sandwich   32

8. Roast Carrot & Harissa Houmous with Pita Bread   36

Mains

9. Butterbean Provençal   42

10. Summer Salad   44

11. Phish Pie   48

12. Beetroot & Mixed Seed Bugers   52

13. Georgian Woodland Mushroom Pasties   56

14. Thai Fab Cakes with Coriander & Lime Mayo   60

15. Beetroot & Sweet Potato Pasties   64

16. Tarka Dahl with Wild Garlic Pakora & Roti   68

17. Linguini Môr Gwyrdd   74

18. Pink Grapefruit & Rocket Salad   76

19. Red & Yellow Pepper Tarte Tatin   78

20. Puglian Potato, Onion & Tomato Casserole   82

21. Bengali Cabbage Curry   86

22. Shiitake Mushroom & Tofu Stir-Fry   90

Desserts

23. Oaty Chocolatey Bonbons   96

24. Jaffa Cakes   98

25. Lemon & Lime Drizzle Cake   100

26. Meadowsweet & Pink Grapefruit Sorbet   103

27. Parsnip, Date & Pecan Cake   106

28. Fruit Cake   110

29. Pineapple, Date & Coconut Crumble   114

30. Whisky Marmalade Bread & Butter Pudding   116

31. Blackberry & Apple Crumble with Custard   120

32. Fruit Scones with Jam & Cream   124

33. Banana & Walnut Loaf with Butterscotch Sauce   128

Breads

34. Pig Farmer's No Knead Baguettes   134

35. Roast Carrot & Sunflower Seed Bread   138

36. Focaccia   142

37. Curry Stuffed Bread Rolls   146

Sauces & Chutneys

38. Fat Hen Pesto   152

39. Elderberry Vinegar   154

40. Aubergine & Apple Chutney   156

41. Spicy Carrot Chutney   158

Metric and imperial equivalents   160

Jane Reynolds

Q: When did you start cooking your own recipes?

A: I started cooking from a very young age and knew that I had a deep fascination for ingredients and how they could be transformed into delicious meals. My paternal grandmother was always cooking and always happy to let me help her; to me, she seemed like a magician.

Q: Have you cooked for others professionally?

A: I started my career as a chef when I was 18, working at The Manor House Hotel, Castle Combe in Wiltshire for 3 years. Missing home, I returned to Pembrokeshire, where I have worked in hotels, restaurants and pubs, including running my own pub and café.

Q: Why did you start to make plant-based/vegan dishes?

A: For most of my career in catering, vegetarian or vegan food was largely ignored. I knew there were great gaps in my knowledge and my curiosity became alive with possible dishes.

I think everyone has the right to choose what they eat for whatever their reasons, whether it be environmental, ethical, or for health benefits. The challenge of thinking outside the box, of extending my knowledge and creating new dishes that were delicious for vegans and non-vegans alike, is what lit my bonfire! I don't want to make my dishes taste or look like meat, I want them to be a celebration of vegetables and plants. Each new dish elates me, and I feel that people who were previously marginalised now have far more choice.

Q: Where do you source your ingredients?

A: Everywhere! I like growing some of my own. I shop in supermarkets, farmers' markets, local shops, farm shops, roadside stalls, online and anywhere else that sells food!

Q: Do you take inspiration from where you live and does foraging influence your cooking?

A: Living in Pembrokeshire, both the land and sea influence me greatly.

Dishes such as linguine môr gwyrdd, phish pie and thai fab cakes are all inspired by the sea. Having been brought up on a farm, where people worked physically hard all day, providing a varied, nutritious and hearty meal was of great importance, so I think that has influenced some of my other creations, such as the curried potato stuffed rolls, beetroot and sweet potato pasties and whisky marmalade bread and butter pudding. Foraging was always part of my life

7

– who doesn't love free food? My grandmother had been brought up in times of great austerity and nothing went to waste. One of my earliest memories of her was picking wild strawberries on a walk at Black Tar, where she lived.

Q: How easy and accessible do you think your recipes are for people first looking to change up their diet?

A: I would like to think that they are all easily accessible, and some really are very simple. Some of the ingredients may be unavailable in all but the larger supermarkets, but all can be found online. Whatever your knowledge or level of experience, I would like to inspire and share my enthusiasm for exploration.

Q: How long does it take you to come up with new plant-based recipes?

A: I find most of my day is taken up with thinking about new recipes, so it doesn't take long to come up with the idea, but sometimes I need to make a dish several times before I'm happy that it fits all the criteria.

Q: Do you think that not being vegan yourself helps you when creating new flavours in your recipes?

A: In a way, I think it does, because if I can make something where I really don't miss meat, fish or dairy, I feel I have succeeded. Often the success of a dish is not just about flavour; texture, nutrition and an aesthetic appeal also play an important part.

Q: What is your go-to ingredient when you're experimenting with new recipes?

A: Chillies, garlic and ginger just go together.

Q: Why do you think that veganism has become so popular in recent years?

A: I think there are many reasons, ranging from ethical and ecological to health benefits. Also, the range of ingredients and the knowledge of how to use them has made it more accessible.

In the past, there was a stigma to a plant-based diet or veganism and some very bad press, but it has become far more mainstream, and vast numbers of people have become interested in the possibilities available to them.

Q: Do you think that this book will be helpful for people who are considering veganism?

A: I don't think anybody should feel any sense of failure if they are only eating plant-based foods part time; many people just want to reduce their intake of meat and dairy, and I'd really like to think that those people would find some inspiration in my book. I think it's all about personal choice, and nobody should be vilified by what they choose to eat or not to eat.

Starters & Sides

Gollops
Fritters &
Ajvar

Gollops (Courgette Fritters)

Makes 6 | Prep time 20 minutes | Cook time 30 minutes

Ingredients

2 tablespoons rapeseed oil
1 large courgette, grated and squeezed, juice discarded
2 onions, finely diced
2 medium carrots, grated
2 spring onions, finely chopped
2 cloves garlic, finely chopped
1 green chilli, finely chopped
1 teaspoon dried mixed herbs (or 2 teaspoons fresh herbs), chopped
1 teaspoon ground cumin
1 teaspoon ground coriander
1 teaspoon turmeric
300g gram flour (besan)
Sea salt and black pepper

I first made these after I had a glut of courgettes in the garden and they were a popular family favourite that acquired the name 'gollops', the reason for which has long been lost in the mists of time!

Method

- Put all the ingredients (except the rapeseed oil) into a large mixing bowl. Combine well and form into 6 fritters.

- Heat the oil in a large heavy-based frying pan. When the oil is hot, add the fritters – don't overcrowd the pan. You will probably need to cook them in 2 batches. After about 2-3 minutes, when the fritters have browned, carefully flip them over. Reduce the heat to medium and cook for 6-7 minutes more. Drain on kitchen paper and keep warm until all the fritters are cooked.

- Serve in a crusty roll with salad and ajvar, or any other spicy sauce or chutney.

Ajvar

Prep time 15 minutes | Cook time 1½ hours

Ingredients

1 large aubergine
3 red peppers
3 medium carrots, topped and tailed, cut into chunks
2 medium onions, quartered
1 long red chilli
1 head garlic
2 tablespoons olive oil
2 teaspoons red wine vinegar
2 teaspoons liquid smoke (optional)
Sea salt and black pepper

Method

- Preheat the oven to 240°C/475°F/Gas 9.

- Put the aubergine and peppers into a roasting tray in the oven for about 30 minutes until they are soft and their skins are blackened and blistering.

- In another roasting tray, put the carrots, onions, unpeeled garlic, chilli pepper (whole) and olive oil. Roast on the bottom shelf, under the aubergines, for 25-30 minutes until soft and caramelised.

- When the aubergines and peppers are done, put into a bowl and cover with cling film. Set aside for 30 minutes or so.

- Squeeze the garlic and chilli from their skins and put them into a food processor with the onion, carrots and the oil in the pan.

Ajvar originated in Serbia but is common in all the Balkan countries with varying recipes.

- Take the top and skin off the aubergine. Peel the peppers, discarding the tops and seeds. Put the aubergine and peppers, along with any cooking liquour, into the food processor.

- Blend all the ingredients until fairly smooth. Tip the contents into a medium-sized saucepan and heat. Add the liquid smoke (if using), vinegar, salt and pepper. Reduce the heat, cover, and let simmer very gently, so that it doesn't stick and burn, for about 1 hour.

- The ajvar should be fairly thick. If it isn't thick enough, increase the heat and cook uncovered, stirring often, until the right consistency is reached.

- Pour into sterilised jars and keep refrigerated.

- Serve with a rustic loaf or flat breads, or as an accompaniment to roast vegetables.

Dolmades &
Taralli Pugliesi

Dolmades

Makes 30 | Prep time 30 minutes | Cook time 45 minutes

Ingredients

40 fresh vine leaves
1 medium onion, finely chopped
1 cup risotto rice
1 medium onion, finely chopped
1 dessertspoon fresh oregano, chopped
1 cup white wine
1 cup vegetable stock
3 tablespoons olive oil
2 bay leaves
½ lemon, juice only
Sea salt and black pepper

Method

• Wash your vine leaves and blanch for a few minutes in boiling water (they will turn a dark green colour). Strain and leave to dry out.

• Meanwhile, make the filling. Sweat off the onions in 1 tablespoon of olive oil for about 2-3 minutes, until transparent but not coloured. Add the rice and oregano. Stir regularly and add the wine and vegetable stock gradually until absorbed by the rice, about 12-15 minutes. Set aside to cool a little.

• Remove the stalks from the vine leaves. Lay the leaves out flat, shiny-side down.

• They are quite fiddly things to fill! Put a teaspoonful of rice at the base (stem end) of each leaf and fold into a parcel – you can patch any holes with a spare leaf.

• Preheat the oven to 200°C/400°F/Gas 6.

Use fresh vine leaves if you can. If you are unable to find fresh, they are available in jars, in which case you wouldn't need to pre-cook them.

- Put your dolmade parcels into the bottom of a round ovenproof pan, approximately 10" (25cm) across. Pack the parcels in tightly so that they don't fall apart when you cook them. Season with sea salt, freshly ground black pepper, lemon juice, 2 tablespoons of olive oil and the bay leaves. Barely cover with water and put an ovenproof plate upside down on top of the dolmades. Put the lid on your pan (or foil, if it doesn't have a lid). Bake in the oven for 30-45 minutes.

- Leave to cool, then refrigerate before serving. Enjoy these as an aperitif with a glass of crisp white wine or as part of a mezze, preferably in the hot sunshine with a sea view!

Taralli Pugliesi

Makes 24 | Prep time 60 minutes | Cook time 45 minutes

Ingredients

250g 'OO' flour
75ml olive oil
100ml white wine
2 generous pinches salt

Optional (to taste):
Freshly ground black pepper
Fennel seeds
Chilli flakes
Onion seeds
Rosemary
Toasted sesame seeds
Poppy seeds

Method

- Mix all the ingredients together in a bowl, including your optional extras, until you have a firm but pliable dough. Knead the dough on a lightly floured surface for about 15 minutes. If you don't feel like doing this, you can knead the dough in a electric mixer with a dough hook, on low speed, for about half the time.

- Cover the dough and leave to rest for a good 30 minutes.

- Once rested, form the taralli by taking a walnut-sized piece of dough and rolling it out with the palm of your hand to make a cord about 1cm thick and 3-4cm long. Form a ring by pressing the ends of the dough together.

- Preheat the oven to 200°C/400°F/Gas 6.

- Bring a saucepan of water to a simmer and add the taralli a few at a time – don't overcrowd them. When they rise to the top of the water, remove with a slotted spoon onto a clean tea towel. Repeat to cook all the taralli.

- When all the taralli have been boiled, place them onto a baking sheet (no need to grease).

- Cook in the oven for 30 minutes until lightly golden brown.

Taralli are common all over southern Italy. They can be kept in an airtight container for a few weeks – if you can resist them for that long!

Tempura
Okra

Tempura Okra with Sweet Chilli Dipping Sauce

Serves 4 | Prep time 20 minutes | Cook time 10 minutes

Ingredients

For the dip:

1 teaspoon cornflour

1 red chilli, finely chopped

1 teaspoon fresh ginger, finely chopped

1 clove garlic, finely chopped

125g golden caster sugar

85ml white wine vinegar

2 teaspoons ume plum seasoning

Pinch salt

1 teaspoon toasted sesame seeds

For the batter:

150g plain flour

100g cornflour

2 teaspoons baking powder

1 teaspoon turmeric

Oil, for deep frying

150g fresh okra

Sea salt

Choose small young okra, as larger older ones can become a bit stringy.

Method

- For the dip, mix the cornflour with a small drop of water to make a paste, making sure all the lumps are dissolved.

- In a small heavy-based saucepan, heat all the other sauce ingredients. Boil for 2 minutes, then add the cornflour mix, stirring continuously so that no lumps form. Reduce to a simmer for a further 3-4 minutes. Pour into a dipping bowl and set aside.

- For the batter, mix the flour, cornflour, baking powder and turmeric together in a large mixing bowl.

- Heat the oil to a high heat in a deep fat fryer or large heavy-based saucepan.

- Toss the okra in the flour mix, tapping off all the excess, and set aside.

- Add enough cold water to the flour mix to form a batter and then add the okra.

- Fry the okra in small batches for about 4-5 minutes and drain on kitchen paper. Sprinkle with salt and serve with the dipping sauce.

Nettle Soup

Serves 4 | Prep time 15 minutes | Cook time 30 minutes

Ingredients

4 medium onions,
chopped
4 medium potatoes,
peeled and chopped
2l vegetable stock
300g freshly picked
young nettles, washed
Sea salt, to taste
White pepper, to taste

Method

- In a large saucepan, combine the onions, potatoes and vegetable stock.

- Bring the mixture to the boil, then reduce to a simmer until the vegetables are soft – this should take around 15-20 minutes.

- Stir in the nettles and bring back to the boil for about 5 minutes.

- Once the nettles are wilted, liquidise the soup, then season with sea salt and white pepper, to taste.

- Serve immediately so the soup retains its vibrant green colour.

Choose young nettle tops and use straight away, as they don't keep long once they have been picked.

Beetroot & Walnut Bread

Makes 8 | Prep time 2½ hours | Cook time 20 minutes

Ingredients

500g strong white flour
14g dried active yeast
12g salt
250g cooked beetroot,
finely chopped
330ml beetroot juice
150g walnuts, chopped

Method

- Mix the flour, yeast and salt in a large mixing bowl. Add the beetroot, beetroot juice and walnuts and stir until combined until you have a soft sticky dough.

- Knead for 5-10 minutes on a well-floured surface.

- Cover the dough and leave to rise for about 2 hours or until doubled in size.

- Tip the dough onto a lightly floured surface and, using a dough scraper to help you, form the dough into a ball and knead softly for 30 seconds.

- Preheat the oven to 230°C/450°F/Gas 8.

- Cut the dough into eight equal pieces. Shape each into a ball and place onto a lightly oiled baking tray. Brush any excess flour off the rolls with a pastry brush. Cover the rolls with a clean tea towel and set aside for about 20 minutes until well risen.

- Bake the rolls for 15-20 minutes until they are well risen and golden and sound hollow when you tap the underside.

If I could blow any myth away it would be that bread making is difficult – it really isn't! It's fun and very satisfying and fills the house with a smell that is every bit as good as the taste.

Peanut Butter

Makes 1 jar | Prep time 5 minutes | Cook time 0 minutes

Ingredients

400g blanched salted
peanuts
2 tablespoons peanut oil
(groundnut oil)

Method

- Put half the peanuts into a food processor and pulse to break them up slightly. Remove and set aside in a mixing bowl.

- Put the remaining nuts into the food processor with the peanut oil and process on full speed until you have a smooth creamy paste.

- Add this to the crushed peanuts in the mixing bowl and stir together.

- Put into a sterilised jam jar and keep in the fridge.

I'm not saying that there is anything wrong in buying peanut butter, but it really is so simple to make. You can of course make it smooth by putting all the peanuts in the food processor.

Gin and Jalapeño Chilli Jam

Prep time 15 minutes | Cook time 1 hour

Ingredients

8 red peppers, pith and seeds removed, roughly chopped

8 red chillies with seeds, roughly chopped

1 thumb-sized piece root ginger

2 large cooking apples, peeled, cored and chopped

6 large cloves garlic

1 (400g) tin chopped tomatoes

2 teaspoons dried chilli flakes

750g golden caster sugar

250ml red wine vinegar

400ml gin

Method

- Put the red peppers, chillies, ginger, apples and garlic into a food processor and blitz well until the ingredients are a pulp.

- Tip the mixture into a large heavy-bottomed saucepan.

- Blitz the tomatoes then add them to the saucepan with the chilli flakes, sugar and vinegar.

- Bring to the boil and skim off any foam that comes to the top.

- Reduce the heat to a simmer and cook for 50-60 minutes.

- After about an hour, turn the heat up and add the gin.

Reuse and recycle old jars of all shapes and sizes to avoid waste.

- Cook for a further 10-15 minutes, stirring regularly so that the jam doesn't stick to the bottom of the pan and burn.

- Transfer into sterilised jars, seal, and leave to cool.

- Label your jars and keep in a cool, dark place for up to 6 months. Refrigerate once opened.

Gin is all the rage, so I've created this fun, fiery and delicious jam, a perfect partner for peanut butter. Put pretty labels and jam pot covers on the pots and give as unusual presents.

Roast Carrot & Harissa Houmous

Serves 4-6 | Prep time 10 minutes | Cook time 40 minutes

Ingredients

2 tablespoons olive oil
6 large carrots, peeled
and cut into chunks
1 onion, diced
1 head garlic, unpeeled,
broken into cloves
1 (400g) tin chickpeas
1 lemon, juice and zest
2 tablespoons olive oil
1 small bunch fresh
coriander, chopped
1 teaspoon ground
cumin
1 tablespoon rose
harissa paste
Sea salt and black
pepper

Method

• Preheat the oven to 220°C/425°F/Gas 7. In a large roasting tray, mix together the carrot chunks, onion and garlic cloves, making sure that everything is well coated with the oil, season with salt and pepper and roast for about 35-40 minutes, or until the carrots are soft and starting to caramelise.

• When the garlic is cool enough to handle, squeeze them out of their skins into a food processor, adding the carrots and all of the oil from the pan.

• Add all the other ingredients, apart from the harissa, and blitz until smooth. Put into a serving dish and swirl through the harissa paste.

• Serve with warm pita breads and a crispy salad.

Pita Bread

Makes 6 | Prep time 3 hours | Cook time 10 minutes

Ingredients

125g wholemeal flour
125g strong white bread flour
5g salt
10g active dried yeast
½ tablespoon olive oil
175ml water

Method

• In a large mixing bowl, combine the flours, salt, and yeast. Add the olive oil and about 125ml of the water. Draw the ingredients together with your hand, adding more water as necessary, until you have a smooth dough.

• Lightly oil your worktop and knead the dough for about 5 minutes. Return the dough to the mixing bowl, cover and set aside for about 2-3 hours or until it is well risen and doubled in size.

• Preheat the oven to 240°C/475°F/Gas 9. Put an upturned baking tray in the oven to preheat.

• On a lightly floured surface, knock the dough back by giving it a quick knead for about 30 seconds. Divide the dough into 6 and allow to rest on the worktop for 15-20 minutes.

Of Middle Eastern origins, pita bread has become popular the world over. Its pocket makes it ideal for a snack food on the go.

- Roll each piece of dough into an oval, 5mm-1cm thick. Dust the preheated baking tray with flour and lay the pitas on the tray – you will probably have to do this in 2 batches.

- Cook in the oven for about 10 minutes until they are puffed up and beginning to brown, then wrap in a clean tea towel to keep them soft. Serve the same day or freeze until they are needed.

If you don't use the pitas on the day they are made, cut into triangle shapes, fry, drain on kitchen roll and use with dips for a starter.

Mains

Butterbean Provençal

Serves 4-6 | Prep time 15 minutes | Cook time 30 minutes

Ingredients

2 tablespoons olive oil
2 onions, finely diced
3 cloves garlic, finely chopped
1 (400g) tin chopped tomatoes
100ml white wine
1 teaspoon capers, chopped
1 tablespoon black olives, chopped
2 (400g) tins butter beans
1 tablespoon mixed fresh herbs, chopped
1 tablespoon tomato purée
Sea salt and black pepper

Method

• In a large heavy-based frying pan, heat 1 tablespoon of the oil, add the onions and garlic and cook over medium heat for 5-10 minutes until they are soft and translucent. Add the tomatoes and white wine and cook for about 10 minutes, stirring occasionally, until the sauce has reduced and thickened.

• Add the capers, olives, butter beans, herbs and tomato purée. Season well with salt and pepper. Cook for a further 5-10 minutes.

• Put into a serving dish and drizzle with the remaining olive oil. Serve hot on a bed of boiled rice or at room temperature with bread and salad.

Vibrant flavours that will take you on a journey to the Mediterranean!

Summer Salad

Summer Salad

Serves 4 | Prep time 15 minutes | Cook time 0 minutes

Ingredients

1 large crispy lettuce
(such as Webb's
Wonderful, romaine,
cos, etc.)
1 red onion, finely sliced
into rings
8-10 radishes, sliced
1 tablespoon fresh mint,
chopped
2 tablespoons mixed
seeds (such as pumpkin,
sunflower, golden
linseed, sesame, hemp,
etc.)
½ cucumber, cut in half
lengthways and thinly
sliced

For the dressing:
1 tablespoon olive oil
2 teaspoons elderberry
vinegar (see p.154) or
balsamic
1 teaspoon golden
caster sugar
1 clove garlic, finely
chopped
Sea salt and black
pepper

I love salad, and it doesn't have to be exotic. My maternal grandfather was a keen gardener and grew lots of vegetables and salad stuff. When I was young, he'd come to the farm every Sunday and always brought whatever was in season – I especially loved the radishes, which were hot and peppery.

Method

- Tear the lettuce into chunks and put into a pretty serving dish. Top with the cucumber, onion, radish, mint and seeds.

- To make the dressing, put the oil, vinegar, sugar, garlic, salt and pepper into a screw topped jar and shake until combined. Check the seasoning and then pour over the salad. Serve straight away so the lettuce stays crisp and crunchy.

Phish Pie

Serves 4 | Prep time 30 minutes | Cook time 40 minutes

Ingredients

For the topping:

1kg potatoes, peeled and chopped into chunks

75ml soya milk

1 tablespoon olive oil

Sea salt and black pepper

1 tablespoon nutritional yeast

1 teaspoon cayenne pepper

For the filling:

1 tablespoon olive oil

2 medium onions, diced

1 celery stalk, finely diced

1 bay leaf

1 teaspoon capers, chopped

1 gherkin (about 25g), diced

50g samphire

2 sprigs fresh tarragon, chopped

1 tablespoon plain flour

250ml white wine

250ml soya milk

125g frozen peas

1 sheet nori, snipped up with scissors

1 (510g) tin banana blossom (I use Chef's Choice – available online)

1 good splash Tabasco

½ lemon, juice only

2 teaspoons ume plum seasoning

Sea salt and black pepper

Method

- Bring the potatoes to the boil in a large saucepan of salted water. Reduce the heat to a simmer and cook for 15-20 minutes until soft, then remove from the heat and drain. Mash with a potato masher until very smooth and no lumps remain. Add the milk, half the olive oil and season well. Set aside.

- Preheat the oven to 220°C/425°F/Gas 7.

- In a large heavy-based frying pan, heat the oil over medium heat and add the onions, celery and bay leaf. Cook for 5-10 minutes, stirring occasionally, until the onions are soft and translucent. Add the capers, gherkin, samphire and tarragon and stir in the flour. Cook gently for 4-5 minutes, stirring often, before slowly adding the wine and milk. Stir continually until a smooth sauce is made.

A traditionally made fish pie is a thing of beauty. I'm very pleased with this no-fish version, which I shan't pretend is exactly the same. Nevertheless, I think it's pretty close, and gives a definite taste of the sea.

- Add the frozen peas and the snipped nori sheet. Keep at a simmer and add the banana blossom, stirring only gently so as not to break it up too much.

- Season with the Tobasco, lemon juice, ume, salt and pepper.

- Pour into an ovenproof pie dish and smooth the potatoes over the top. Make a nice pattern with a fork and drizzle with the rest of the olive oil. Sprinkle on the nutritional yeast and cayenne pepper.

- Bake in the oven for 30-40 minutes until the top is golden brown.

- Serve with a crisp green salad or a selection of fresh vegetables.

Beetroot and Mixed Seed Burgers

Beetroot and Mixed Seed Burgers

Serves 8 | Prep time 30 minutes | Cook time 30 minutes

Ingredients

1 tablespoon olive oil
2 medium onions, finely diced
2 cloves garlic, finely chopped
200g mixed seeds (sunflower, pumpkin, golden linseed, hemp)
75g rolled oats
3 medium beetroots (about 425g), topped but unpeeled, roughly chopped
1 teaspoon ground coriander
1 teaspoon ground cumin
1 teaspoon chilli powder
1 bunch fresh parsley, chopped
1 tablespoon tomato ketchup
2 replacement eggs (I use Orgran No Egg Egg Replacer, available in healthfood shops or online)
Sea salt and black pepper
Rapeseed oil, for frying

The stunning colour of these burgers is not the only thing they have going for them! They are delicious and very nutritious too.

Method

- In a large heavy-based frying pan, heat the oil and gently fry the onions and garlic for 5-10 minutes until soft and translucent.

- Put the rolled oats and 150g of the mixed seeds into a food processor and whizz to a coarse meal consistency. Transfer to a large mixing bowl.

- Whizz the beetroot up until well chopped but not puréed. Add to the mixing bowl with the other ingredients, including the 50g of whole seeds, stir and season well.

- Divide into 8 and squeeze together to make patties.

- Heat a tablespoon of rapeseed oil in a large heavy-based frying pan and fry the patties in batches for about 5 minutes on each side.

- Serve in fresh homemade rolls with crisp salad, homemade onion rings or sliced beef tomatoes.

Georgian Woodland Mushroom Pasties

Georgian Woodland Mushroom Pasties

Serves 8 | Prep time 2 hours | Cook time 30 minutes

Ingredients

500g strong white bread flour
360ml lukewarm water
12g dried active yeast
10g salt

For the filling:
1 tablespoon rapeseed oil
2 medium onions, finely diced
2 cloves garlic, finely diced
300g chestnut mushrooms, finely diced
250g mixed woodland mushrooms, roughly chopped
1 teaspoon dried mixed herbs
1 small bunch flat-leaf parsley, chopped
250g cooked rice
Sea salt and black pepper
Rapeseed oil, for frying

These pasties conjure up autumnal images of foraging; they would make a great picnic snack to take along with you.

Method

- In a large mixing bowl, combine the flour, yeast, salt and water to make a dough. Cover and set aside in a warm place for about 2 hours or until doubled in size.

- In the meantime, heat the oil in a large heavy-based frying pan over medium to high heat. Sauté the onions and garlic for a few minutes until translucent and then add the mushrooms and mixed herbs. Season well with plenty of salt and pepper. Cook for a further 3-4 minutes. Stir in the parsley and set aside to cool.

- When the mixture is cold, stir in the rice.

- When the dough has risen, tip it onto a floured worktop. Divide into 8. Roll each piece into a circle and divide the filling equally between them.

- Dab the edges of each pasty with a drop of water to help seal. Fold each one over to make a pasty and squeeze the edges together.

- Pour about 1 tablespoon of rapeseed oil into a large non-stick frying pan over medium to high heat. Fry each pasty for about 8 minutes, turning halfway through so that they are nice and golden on both sides. Serve hot.

Thai Fab Cakes with Coriander and Lime Mayonnaise

Serves 4 | Prep time 30 minutes | Cook time 20 minutes

Ingredients

500g potatoes, peeled and cut into chunks
½ tablespoon olive oil
½ tablespoon soya milk
Sea salt and white pepper
1 (220g drained weight) tin hearts of palm, sliced into chunks and shredded
2 cloves garlic, chopped
½ tablespoon fresh ginger, chopped
1 stalk lemongrass, chopped
3 spring onions, chopped

1 small bunch fresh coriander
1 tablespoon olive oil
½ lime, juice only
Sea salt
100g breadcrumbs
Sunflower oil, for frying

For the mayonnaise:
120ml unsweetened soya milk (room temperature)
240ml vegetable oil
1 tablespoon olive oil
2 teaspoons white wine vinegar

2 teaspoons maple syrup
½ lemon, juice only
Dash Tabasco
Sea salt and black pepper
1 lime, juice and zest
1 small bunch fresh coriander, chopped

Method

- Boil the potatoes in a saucepan of salted water for about 10 minutes until soft. Strain and mash with the olive oil, soya milk and white pepper. Set aside to cool.

- In a blender, mix together the garlic, ginger, lemongrass, spring onions, coriander, oil, lime juice and salt. Blend to a smooth purée.

- In a large mixing bowl, combine the cooled mashed potatoes, shredded palm hearts and the paste. Divide into 4 patties.

- Put the breadcrumbs onto a plate and coat the patties in crumbs.

- To make the mayonnaise, put the milk, oils, vinegar, maple syrup, lemon juice and Tabasco into a jug. Then, with a stick blender, whizz to a

Well, I have to say that I had lots of laughs trying to name these Thai 'crab' cakes – some of the rhymes not being entirely favourable!

mayonnaise. Season well and stir in the lime juice and zest and the coriander.

- In a large heavy-based frying pan, heat about 2 tablespoons of oil over medium to high heat. Add the patties and cook for about 5 minutes until browned. Carefully turn over and brown on the other side for about 3-4 minutes, then reduce the heat to low to medium and cook for another 2-3 minutes.

- Serve with the mayonnaise, lime wedges and fresh spicy salad leaves.

Beetroot & Sweet Potato Pasties

Beetroot & Sweet Potato Pasties

Serves 4 | Prep time 20 minutes | Cook time 1 hour

Ingredients

375g rolled puff pastry
1 tablespoon olive oil
2 medium beetroots,
peeled and diced
2 medium sweet
potatoes, peeled and
diced
6 cloves garlic, unpeeled
2 medium onions, finely
diced
½ red chilli pepper, finely
diced
2 teaspoons dried herbs
Sea salt and black
pepper
1 tablespoon soya milk

Method

• Preheat oven to 200°C/400°F/Gas 6.

• In a large roasting tray, combine the oil, beetroot, sweet potatoes, garlic, onions, chilli, mixed herbs, salt and pepper. Roast in the oven for about 40-45 minutes – the vegetables should be soft and caramelising around the edges. Allow to cool.

• Squeeze the garlic from their skins and stir into the vegetables.

• Take the pastry from the fridge and unroll. I find it easier to leave it on the paper that it comes with, as it's less likely to stick or tear. Cut into quarters.

• Put about a tablespoonful of vegetable mixture onto one half of each of the rectangles. Brush the soya milk in a horseshoe shape around the filled side of the pastry.

- Fold the other side over the filling and press down to seal the edges. Then, using a fork, press down gently right the way around the pastry to seal it well. Brush the top of each pasty with a little soya milk and prod the top 2-3 times with a fork to allow the steam to escape during cooking.

- Transfer to a lightly oiled baking tray and bake for approximately 20 minutes until risen and golden.

- Serve hot or cold.

These are great for lunchboxes and picnics. I have made them on several occasions and I am always complimented on them.

Roti

Serves 6 | Prep time 1½ hours | Cook time 15 minutes

Ingredients

225g self-raising flour
½ teaspoon salt
1 tablespoon olive oil,
plus extra for brushing
Vegetable oil, for frying

Method

- Put the flour and salt into a large mixing bowl, adding the olive oil and enough water to make a soft dough. Knead gently until smooth, then cover and leave to rest for 30 minutes.

- Divide the dough into 6 and roll each piece into circles, each the thickness of a coin. Brush the bottom third of each with olive oil and fold this towards the middle of the dough. Brush the unfolded piece with oil and fold this on top of the folded dough. Turn 90 degrees and repeat the process of oiling and folding, then leave to rest for 30 minutes.

- Heat a heavy-based frying pan, unoiled. Roll each roti as thinly as possible and place into the pan one at a time.

- Once the roti starts to puff up with brown flecks, turn over to cook on the other side. They should cook in 1-2 minutes, depending on thickness.

Wild Garlic Pakoras

Serves 4-6 | Prep time 15 minutes | Cook time 30 minutes

Ingredients

1 tablespoon rapeseed oil
1 teaspoon black onion seeds
1 teaspoon black cumin seeds or nigella seeds
2 medium onions, finely diced
2 medium potatoes, peeled and finely diced
1 green chilli, finely diced
½ lemon, juice only
150g wild garlic, washed, blanched and chopped
300g chickpea flour (besan)

1 teaspoon chilli powder
1 teaspoon salt
1 teaspoon garam masala
Vegetable or sunflower oil, for deep frying

The smell of wild garlic transports me back in time to my childhood. My father and mother used to love 'going out for a run' in the car, the narrow lanes filled with wildflowers, and in early spring the scent of the wild garlic as we drove along was heady.

Method

- In a heavy-based frying pan, heat the rapeseed oil and add the onion seeds and cumin seeds. Fry gently for a few moments before adding the onions, potatoes and green chilli.

- Cook slowly for about 15 minutes, stirring occasionally, until the potato is soft. Add the lemon juice and allow to cool, then set aside.

- In a large mixing bowl, combine the chickpea flour, chilli powder, salt and garam masala.

- Mix in the wild garlic and the potato mixture, then combine together with just enough water to create a stiff batter.

- Heat the oil in a deep fat fryer (to about 175ºC) or large saucepan. When the oil is hot, drop in tablespoonfuls of the batter. Cook in batches to avoid overcrowding.

- Cook for a few minutes until golden, then flip them over to cook on the other side. When they are golden all over, remove with a slotted spoon onto kitchen paper to drain.

- Serve hot and crispy.

Tarka Dahl

Serves 4-6 | Prep time 20 minutes | Cook time 30 minutes

Ingredients

500g red split lentils, picked over and rinsed
2 teaspoons turmeric
1 teaspoon ground cumin
2 cloves garlic, peeled and finely chopped
Thumb-sized piece of ginger, finely chopped
1 teaspoon chilli flakes
1 teaspoon ground coriander
5 green cardamom pods
Pinch dried curry leaves
1 vegetable stock cube
500ml water
1 tablespoon rapeseed oil

2 teaspoons panch phoron
3 medium onions, finely sliced
2-3 green jalapeño chillies, finely sliced
2 vine ripened tomatoes, thinly sliced
1 small bunch fresh coriander, chopped
3-4 mint leaves
Sea salt and black pepper

I first started making this years ago, when I was introduced to it whilst babysitting for an Indian couple.

Method

- Add the lentils, tumeric, cumin, garlic, ginger, chilli flakes, coriander, cardamom pods, curry leaves, stock cube and water (the lentils should be covered by about an inch of water) to a large heavy-based saucepan and cover. Bring to the boil then reduce the heat to a simmer for about 30 minutes, stirring occasionally, until the dahl has the consistency of thick vegetable soup. Add a little more water if necessary.

- While the dahl is cooking, make your tarka. Heat the oil in a frying pan, add the panch phoron and cook for a few minutes, then add the onion.

- Fry the onions until they start to brown, then add the chillies and sliced tomatoes. Cook for about 2-3 minutes, stirring often, then stir in the chopped coriander.

- When the dahl is cooked, check the seasoning, then put into a pretty serving dish, top with the tarka and garnish with the mint leaves.

Brought up on the Pembrokeshire coastline, the sea has been a huge influence on my life. This dish is one of the ones I am most proud of.

Linguine Môr Gwyrdd

Serves 4 | Prep time 15 minutes | Cook time 15 minutes

Ingredients

400g dried linguine
2 tablespoons olive oil
2 green chillies
4 spring onions, sliced
on the diagonal
120g samphire
1½ tablespoons capers,
chopped
2 cloves garlic, finely
chopped
2 tablespoons
laverbread (or 2 sheets
nori, torn)
Sea salt and black
pepper

Method

- Cook the linguine according to the packet instructions, keeping it *al dente*. Once cooked, strain.

- While the pasta is cooking, make the sauce. In a heavy-based frying pan, gently heat the oil over medium heat.

- Add the chillies and spring onions and sauté for 1-2 minutes, stirring regularly. Add the samphire, capers and garlic, stirring continually whilst they cook, for 2-3 minutes.

- Add the laverbread (or nori), heat through for a minute, then check the seasoning (don't forget that the capers may be quite salty already, so be careful not to over season).

- Stir in the linguine, divide between 4 hot pasta dishes and serve immediately.

Pink Grapefruit & Rocket Salad

Serves 2 | Prep time 15 minutes | Cook time 0 minutes

Ingredients

1 pink grapefruit
1-2 little gem lettuces
1 large handful rocket
100g roasted walnuts
2 tablespoons extra
virgin olive oil
1 tablespoon balsamic
or elderberry vinegar
(see p.154)
Sea salt and black
pepper

Method

- Remove the peel and pith of the grapefruit and segment by cutting between the membranes. Squeeze out the juice from the remains of the grapefruit.

- Whisk together the olive oil and elderberry or balsamic vinegar, the grapefruit juice, salt and black pepper, to taste.

- Tear the lettuce and put into a pretty serving dish. Pile on the rocket and arrange the grapefruit segments on top. Drizzle on the vinaigrette, scatter on the walnuts and serve.

Summery, pretty, peppery and packed with flavour.

Red & Yellow Pepper Tarte Tatin

Red & Yellow Pepper Tarte Tatin

Serves 4 | Prep time 60 minutes | Cook time 35 minutes

Ingredients

For the pastry:
250g plain flour
125g non-dairy butter
Pinch salt
3-4 tablespoons cold
water

For the filling:
3 tablespoons olive oil
4 peppers, 2 red and 2
yellow, quartered,
stems, seeds and pith
removed
3 onions, finely sliced
3 cloves garlic, finely
chopped
25g golden caster sugar
2 tablespoons balsamic
vinegar

25g pine nuts
Handful fresh basil
leaves, torn
Sea salt and black pepper

Method

• To make the pastry, rub the butter into the flour
  until it resembles fine breadcrumbs. Add the salt.

• Add 3-4 tablespoons of cold water and bring
  together until you have a soft dough. Wrap
  the dough in cling film and refrigerate whilst
  preparing the filling.

• Heat the oil in an ovenproof frying pan over
  medium heat and add the peppers. Reduce the
  heat a little to medium-low and cook the peppers,
  turning from time to time, for about 30 minutes.

- Remove the peppers from the pan using a slotted spoon and set aside.

- Preheat the oven to 220°C/425°F/Gas 7. Add the caster sugar and balsamic vinegar to the pan and let it bubble over medium heat for about 3-4 minutes, then add the onions and garlic. Cook slowly over medium to low heat for about 20 minutes. Stir in the pine nuts.

- Remove the onions with a slotted spoon and set aside.

- Arrange the peppers in the bottom of the pan, skin-side down, alternating the colours. Cover the peppers with the onions.

- On a floured worktop, roll out the pastry into a circle about 2.5cm larger in diameter than your pan with the peppers in.

- Arrange the pastry on top of the peppers and onions, tucking the excess down the sides of the pan. Prick 2-3 small holes in the pastry to allow the steam to escape during cooking.

- Cook in the oven for 35 minutes or until the pastry is golden brown.

- Place an inverted plate on top of the pastry and turn the pan over to tip the tart out. Scatter with the torn basil leaves, sea salt and black pepper.

Puglian Potato, Onion & Tomato Casserole

Puglian Potato, Onion & Tomato Casserole

Serves 4 | Prep time 15 minutes | Cook time 60 minutes

Ingredients

3 medium potatoes, peeled and sliced

3 medium onions, peeled and sliced

3 vine-ripened tomatoes, sliced

3 cloves garlic, finely chopped

2-3 sprigs fresh oregano

Sea salt and black pepper

1½ tablespoons Puglian olive oil

Approximately 400ml vegetable stock

Breadcrumbs

Method

• Preheat the oven to 180°C/350°F/Gas 4.

• Grease a terracotta baking dish with a little olive oil. If you don't have a terracotta dish, any deep ovenproof dish will do.

• Place a layer of sliced onion on the bottom of the dish and drizzle with olive oil. Next, add a layer of potato then a layer of tomato. Sprinkle with garlic, oregano leaves, salt, pepper and another drizzle of olive oil.

• Repeat the layers until all the ingredients are used up. On the top layer, make an attractive pattern with the potatoes and tomatoes.

• Add enough vegetable stock to come about halfway up the dish.

Use the very best ingredients that you can for this recipe. For such a simple dish, the flavours are incredible.

- Sprinkle the top with breadcrumbs and another drizzle of olive oil.

- Bake for 45-60 minutes until all the ingredients are cooked through, the top is nicely browned and most of the liquid has been absorbed by the vegetables.

- Let the casserole stand for 10 minutes or so before serving.

Bengali Cabbage Curry

Bengali Cabbage Curry

Serves 4 | Prep time 15 minutes | Cook time 30 minutes

Ingredients

1 tablespoon rapeseed oil

2 teaspoons panch phoron

3 cloves

2 bay leaves

1 large onion, diced

3 cloves garlic, finely chopped

½ scotch bonnet chilli, finely diced

1 small thumb-sized piece of ginger, finely chopped

250g sweetheart cabbage, finely shredded

2 medium potatoes, peeled and diced

1 (400g) tin chopped tomatoes

1 teaspoon ground coriander

1 teaspoon ground cumin

1 teaspoon turmeric

1 vegetable stock cube, dissolved in 200ml boiling water

2 tablespoons coconut milk

Sea salt and black pepper

1 small bunch fresh coriander, torn

Who would have thought it?
Cabbage curry! But believe me, this
is an absolute revelation.

Method

- In a large heavy-based frying pan, heat the oil and fry the panch phoron for about a minute until the seeds pop and their aroma is released. Add the cloves and bay leaves, stir, then add the onion, garlic, chilli and ginger. Fry gently, stirring occasionally, for about 3-4 minutes.

- Add the cabbage and potato and cook on medium heat for 3-4 minutes more.

- Add the chopped tomatoes, coriander, cumin, turmeric and vegetable stock. Simmer for 15-20 minutes until the potatoes are soft.

- Stir in the coconut milk and season.

- Garnish with fresh coriander and serve with boiled rice, roti or naan bread.

Shiitake Mushroom & Tofu Stir-Fry

Shiitake Mushroom & Tofu Stir-Fry

Serves 4 | Prep time 20 minutes | Cook time 10 minutes

Ingredients

For the marinade:
1½ tablespoons sesame oil
2 teaspoons toasted sesame seeds
3 teaspoons yakitori sauce
3 teaspoons Shoaxing rice wine
2 teaspoons maple syrup
1 teaspoon Chinese five spice
125g shiitake mushrooms

For the stir fry:
1 tablespoon rapeseed oil
3 medium onions, diced
2 cloves garlic, finely chopped
½ long red chilli, finely diced
Thumb-sized piece of ginger, finely chopped
1 (396g) pack firm tofu, drained and pressed
100g baby corn
125g white cabbage, finely sliced

2 spring onions, finely sliced
100g mange tout
2 teaspoons cornflour
200ml vegetable stock (or 1 stock cube, dissolved in 200ml boiling water)
Sea salt and black pepper

I love stir fries, they're a great way to celebrate the huge and diverse choice of vegetables available to us. To complete the experience, chopsticks are a must!

Method

- Mix all the marinade ingredients together, pour over the mushrooms and set aside.

- Heat the oil in a wok. When it is sizzling, add the onions, garlic, chilli and ginger and stir constantly for about 5 minutes. Once the onions have started to soften, add the tofu and stir-fry for 2 minutes, then add the corn, white cabbage and spring onions. Stir constantly for 2 minutes more, then add the mushrooms and mange tout.

- Gradually add the stock to the cornflour, stirring to make a paste.

- Pour in the vegetable stock and the cornflour and cook for a further 2-3 minutes. Check the seasoning.

- Serve hot with Chinese noodles or boiled rice.

Desserts

Oaty Chocolate Bonbons

Makes 20 | Prep time 15 minutes | Cooling time 4 hours

Ingredients

100g golden caster
sugar
50g coconut oil
or dairy-free butter
50ml almond milk,
or other non-dairy milk
35g cocoa powder
175g rolled oats
25g mixed nuts,
chopped
25g raisins, chopped
8 glacé cherries,
chopped
½ teaspoon almond
essence

Method

- Put the sugar, coconut oil, milk and cocoa powder into a medium-sized heavy-based saucepan and gently bring to the boil, stirring often. Reduce the heat to a simmer and cook for 2-3 minutes, minding that it doesn't stick and burn.

- Remove from the heat and stir in the oats, nuts, raisins, cherries and almond essence. Allow to cool. (This is not essential, but it makes the next step easier.)

- With 2 teaspoons, quenelle the mixture into approximately 20 balls. Place onto a very lightly greased plate and refrigerate for at least 4 hours.

- If you haven't got a very good quenelle technique, you could spoon the mixture into petit cases.

- Enjoy with a coffee or as part of an afternoon tea.

Jaffa Cakes

Makes 12-15 | Prep time 10 minutes | Cook time 15 minutes

Ingredients

100g self-raising flour
60g golden caster sugar
100ml soya milk
50ml rapeseed oil
1 teaspoon vanilla
essence
200g dark chocolate
50g dairy-free butter
100g orange marmalade
(smooth, without rind)

Method

• Preheat the oven to 180°C/350°F/Gas 4.

• Mix the flour and sugar together, add the soya milk, oil and vanilla essence and stir until just combined into a batter.

• Drop a small spoonful of the batter into each hole of a fairy cake tin. Bake in the oven for 8-10 minutes until just coloured and firm. Allow to cool in the tin for 1-2 minutes before removing to a cooling rack.

• Melt the chocolate and butter together in a medium-sized saucepan over low heat, stirring often.

• When the bases have cooled, spoon a teaspoonful of marmalade onto each one.

• Coat each cake with chocolate and refrigerate for at least 4 hours before serving. Keep refrigerated.

Lemon & Lime Drizzle Cake

Lemon & Lime Drizzle Cake

Makes 1 cake | Prep time 15 minutes | Cook time 30 minutes

Ingredients

For the cake:

275g self-raising flour
1 teaspoon baking powder
200g golden caster sugar
100ml vegetable oil
1 lemon, juice and zest
1 lime, juice and zest
150ml cold water
1 teaspoon yellow food colouring (optional)

For the topping:

100g golden caster sugar
1 lemon, juice and zest
1 lime, juice and zest

Method

• Preheat the oven to 180°C/350°F/Gas 4.

• Mix the flour, baking powder and sugar together in a large mixing bowl.

• Add the oil, lemon and lime juices, the water and the food colouring, if using. Mix together well until the cake batter is smooth, pour into a lined loaf tin and bake for approximately 30 minutes or until a skewer inserted in the middle of the cake comes out clean. Leave in the tin.

• To make the topping, mix all the topping ingredients together.

• With a skewer, make several holes in the top of the cake so that the topping mixture can seep into it. Pour on the topping and allow the loaf to cool in the tin before turning out.

Meadowsweet & Pink Grapefruit Sorbet

Serves 6 | Prep time 30 minutes | Freezing time 3 days

Ingredients

About 40 meadowsweet
flowers, stalks removed
600ml water
225g golden caster
sugar
1 lemon, juice only
1 pink grapefruit, juice
and flesh

Method

- Remove as much of the stalk from the meadowsweet flowers as you can, as they can impart a slight medicinal taste.

- In a medium-sized saucepan, bring the water and sugar to the boil then reduce to a simmer, stirring occasionally, until you have a light syrup, about 10 minutes.

- Take the syrup off the heat, add the lemon juice, grapefruit juice and flesh and the meadowsweet flowers. Stir, then cover and leave to cool completely.

- Once completely cooled, strain the liquid into a bowl through a muslin cloth or tea towel.

- Cover the bowl and freeze for about 12 hours, then whizz with a stick blender until creamy. Return to the freezer for a further 24 hours.

- Repeat the blending process and return to the freezer for a couple of days before eating.

- The sorbet goes a long way due to its highly fragranced taste, so serve small amounts with pink grapefruit segments, garnished with a mint or basil leaf.

Parsnip, Date & Pecan Cake

Parsnip, Date and Pecan Cake

Makes 1 cake | Prep time 20 minutes | Cook time 45 minutes

Ingredients

For the cake:
400g parsnips, peeled
and cut into cubes
100ml apple juice
2 tablespoons maple
syrup
275g self-raising flour
1 teaspoon baking
powder
1 teaspoon mixed spice
175g dairy-free butter
150g golden caster sugar
1 teaspoon vanilla
essence
150g dried dates,
chopped
100g pecans, chopped
2 chunks stem ginger in
syrup, finely chopped

For the topping:
250g icing sugar
2 tablespoons maple
syrup
1 tablespoon syrup from
the jar of stem ginger
8 whole pecans

Method

- Put the parsnips and the apple juice in a medium-sized saucepan, cover and bring to the boil. Once boiling, reduce the heat to a simmer and cook for about 10 minutes, stirring occasionally, until the parsnip is very soft.

- Remove the lid and keep on low heat until only a small amount of liquid remains. Pour over the maple syrup, mash, and set aside.

- Grease and line a 24cm round cake tin with baking parchment or greaseproof paper.

- Preheat the oven to 180°C/350°F/Gas 4.

- Sift the flour, baking powder and mixed spice together in a large mixing bowl.

- Beat the butter, sugar and vanilla essence together in a separate bowl until light and creamy. Add this to the parsnip mash with the dates, dried pecans and ginger and stir until everything is combined.

- Transfer the mixture to the prepared baking tin and bake in the oven for 40-45 minutes until a skewer inserted into the middle of the cake comes out clean. Turn out onto a cooling rack and allow to cool completely.

- To make the topping, sift the icing sugar into a large mixing bowl and stir in the syrups. Pour over the cold cake and smooth with a palette knife, allowing some to run over the sides a little. Decorate with the whole pecans.

Fruit Cake

Fruit Cake

Makes 1 cake | Prep time 12 hours | Cook time 1¼ hours

Ingredients

1kg dried mixed fruit
(which in the main
should be sultanas,
currants, raisins and
mixed peel, but can also
include glacé cherries,
dried cranberries, figs,
dates, apricots, etc.)
100g mixed nuts,
chopped
50g mixed seeds
(optional)
700ml soya milk
350g self-raising flour
1 tablespoon orange
marmalade
1-2 tablespoons sherry,
rum, brandy or whisky
Icing sugar, to dust

Method

- Put the fruit, nuts and seeds in a large mixing bowl and pour over the soya milk. Leave to soak in the fridge overnight.

- Preheat the oven to 160°C/325°F/Gas 3. Line a 24cm springform cake tin with baking parchment or greaseproof paper.

- When the fruit has soaked, stir in the flour and marmalade – the batter will be quite stiff. Put the cake mix into your prepared tin and bake for approximately 1¼ hours, or until a skewer inserted in the middle of the cake comes out clean.

- Brush the surface of the cake with your chosen liquor, allow it to soak in and repeat until all the liquor is used up.

- When the cake is cold, turn out of the tin onto a cake stand and dust with icing sugar.

This is just such a great cake! You could easily make it into a Christmas cake by covering it in marzipan and decorating with icing.

Pineapple, Date & Coconut Crumble

Serves 6 | Prep time 30 minutes | Cook time 40 minutes

Ingredients

For the filling:

300g fresh pineapple,
peeled and chopped
175g dates, roughly
chopped
175g dried apricots,
roughly chopped
100g golden sultanas
4-5 cardamoms, crushed
250ml white wine
200ml water

For the crumble:

100g desiccated coconut
100g Demerara sugar
100g non-dairy butter
100g plain flour
1 teaspoon mixed spice

Method

• Preheat the oven to 190°C/375°F/Gas 5.

• Place all the filling ingredients in a large pan and simmer for 30 minutes until the liquid is reduced by at least half. Pour into a pie dish.

• Rub all the crumble ingredients together and spoon over the filling mix. Cook in the oven for about 40 minutes until golden brown and bubbling around the edges. Serve with ice cream or custard.

This is a lovely alternative to the traditional crumble.

Whisky Marmalade Bread & Butter Pudding

Whisky Marmalade Bread & Butter Pudding

Serves 4-6 | Prep time 20 minutes | Cook time 35 minutes

Ingredients

½ loaf slightly stale white farmhouse bread, thickly sliced
175g non-dairy butter
175g marmalade
2 tablespoons cornflour
500ml soya milk
100g golden caster sugar
100ml whisky
1 teaspoon vanilla essence

For the topping:
50g golden caster sugar
½ teaspoon ground mixed spice

Method

• Remove any hard crusts from the bread. Spread with the butter and marmalade, cut the slices in half and layer in an ovenproof dish. Preheat the oven to 200°C/400°F/Gas 6.

• Mix a little of the milk into the cornflour to make a smooth paste.

• Heat the rest of the milk in a medium-sized heavy-based saucepan until almost boiling, remove from the heat and pour onto the cornflour mixture, stirring continuously.

• Return to the saucepan and bring to a simmer over low to medium heat, stirring often. After 2-3 minutes, add the sugar, whisky and vanilla essence. Cook very gently for a further 3-4 minutes.

Whisky elevates the humble bread and butter pudding to a whole new level!

- Pour over the bread, butter and marmalade, sprinkle with the sugar and mixed spice for the topping and bake in the oven for 30-35 minutes, until golden brown and bubbling.

- Allow to cool for 10 minutes. Serve with ice cream or custard.

Blackberry & Apple Crumble with custard

Going blackberry picking for me is another lovely childhood memory. My grandmother, who had grown up and lived through times of great austerity, made use of all the free food she could gather. She made jam, crumble and tarts and transformed seemingly ordinary ingredients into something fantastic that we would always nag her to make again and again.

Blackberry & Apple Crumble

Serves 6 | Prep time 15 minutes | Cook time 45 minutes

Ingredients

For the topping:
400g flour
200g porridge oats
150g golden caster sugar
200g dairy-free butter
1 teaspoon ground mixed spice

For the filling:
750g blackberries
4 medium Bramley apples, peeled, cored and sliced
100g golden caster sugar
150ml orange juice

Method

- Preheat the oven to 200°C/400°F/Gas 6.

- To make the topping, sift the flour into a bowl and add the oats, sugar, butter and spices and rub together until you have an even crumbly mixture.

- Combine the sugar, blackberries and apples and add to a large ovenproof dish. Pour over the orange juice, then top with the crumble mixture, spreading gently until you have an even layer covering all the fruit.

- Bake in the oven for about 40-45 minutes until the topping is golden brown and the fruit is soft. Serve with custard or soya yoghurt.

Custard

Serves 6 | Prep time 5 minutes | Cook time 10 minutes

Ingredients

1l soya milk
3 tablespoons cornflour
3 tablespoons golden caster sugar
1 teaspoon vanilla essence
Yellow food colouring
1 large piece ginger (optional)

Method

- In a mixing bowl, gradually add the milk to the cornflour, whisking all the time so that no lumps remain. Transfer to a medium-sized saucepan with the sugar and vanilla essence.

- Heat gently over a medium heat, whisking until the custard thickens. Simmer for 5-10 minutes until the cornflour has cooked out, stirring regularly to prevent it from sticking and burning.

- Check the sweetness – you may want to add a little more sugar if you prefer a sweeter custard. Add the yellow food colouring a drop at a time until you have the desired colour.

- **For ginger custard:** Follow the recipe above to stage 2, then grate a large thumb-sized piece of ginger, squeeze the juice into the milk, put the pulp into a small muslin bag or tie into a piece of cotton cloth and add to the milk. Continue with the recipe, removing the ginger just before serving.

Fruit Scones with Jam & Cream

Fruit Scones with Jam & Cream

Serves 6 | Prep time 15 minutes | Cook time 20 minutes

Ingredients

For the scones:

250g self-raising flour
50g non-dairy butter
50g golden caster sugar
Pinch salt
50g dried fruit (sultanas, raisins, cranberries, cherries, apricots, etc.)
100ml soya milk

For the topping:

1 (400g) tin full-fat coconut milk, stored overnight in the fridge
Jam of your choice

Method

• Preheat the oven to 220°C/425°F/Gas 7. Put the flour and butter into a medium-sized mixing bowl and rub together to make a fine breadcrumb consistency.

• Stir in the sugar, salt and fruit, then add the milk. With your hand, bring all the ingredients together to make a soft dough.

• Tip the dough onto a lightly floured surface and roll to about 2cm thick. Then, with a pastry cutter, cut out your scones. Squeeze together the remaining dough mixture then roll out and cut again. You should have about 6-7 scones.

• Put the scones on a baking sheet lined with baking parchment or greaseproof paper and bake for about 15-20 minutes until risen and golden brown.

- Cool on a cooling rack.

- To make the cream, drain the water from the tin of coconut milk, tip the solids into a small mixing bowl and whisk with an electric hand whisk until you have a whipped cream consistency.

- Cut the scones in half and top with jam and cream.

Banana & Walnut Loaf with Butterscotch Sauce

Banana & Walnut Loaf with Butterscotch Sauce

Makes 1 cake | Prep time 20 minutes | Cook time 50 minutes

Ingredients

For the loaf:

5 bananas
75g non-dairy butter
150g soft light brown sugar
125g non-dairy yoghurt
½ teaspoon salt
175g self-raising flour
1 teaspoon bicarbonate of soda
50g walnuts, chopped
1 teaspoon vanilla essence

You can serve this hot or cold, it's delicious either way.

For the sauce:

125g soft light brown sugar
100g non-dairy butter
200ml coconut milk
1 teaspoon vanilla essence
1 teaspoon salt

Method

- Preheat the oven to 180°C/350°F/Gas 4. Line a 2lb (900g) loaf tin with baking parchment or greaseproof paper.

- In a medium-sized mixing bowl, add 3 of the bananas and mash to a soft paste with a fork or masher. Add the other 2 bananas and crush, but leave some lumps for texture. Set aside.

- In a large mixing bowl, whisk together the butter and sugar until it is light and fluffy. Add the yoghurt and salt and beat again until well combined.

- Fold in the flour, bicarbonate of soda, bananas, walnuts and vanilla essence.

- Pour into the prepared loaf tin and bake for about 50 minutes until a skewer inserted in the middle of the cake comes out clean.

- Leave the cake in the tin whilst you prepare the sauce.

- To make the sauce, mix all the ingredients in a medium-sized saucepan over medium heat. Stir until everything has melted and combined together.

- Turn the banana cake out onto a serving plate and serve with a jug of the butterscotch sauce.

Breads

Pig Farmer's No Knead Baguettes

Pig Farmer's No Knead Baguettes

Makes 3 baguettes | Prep time 2 hours | Cook time 20 minutes

Ingredients

400g T55 flour
10g dried active yeast
10g salt
350ml lukewarm water
1-2l very cold water

Method

• Weigh out the flour, yeast and salt in a large mixing bowl and mix together. Make a well in the centre and add the 350ml of lukewarm water. Mix with a metal spoon to form a dough (the dough will be quite wet). Cover and leave to rise for about 2 hours or until doubled in size.

• Tip the dough out onto a well-floured worktop and use a dough scraper to help slice the dough into 3 equal parts. Shape each ball into a baguette shape and place on a lightly greased baguette tray. (You can buy baguette trays online or from cookware shops.)

• Preheat the oven to 250°C/475°F/Gas 9. Have a baking tray in the bottom of the oven ready to pour in about 1-2l of very cold water when your bread is ready to bake.

- In the meantime, allow the dough to rise again in a warm place for about 20 minutes.

- When risen, if you have a very sharp knife, you can score the tops of the baguettes if you like.

- Fill your tray in the oven with the very cold water and bake the baguettes for 15-20 minutes until well risen and golden. The bread should sound hollow when tapped underneath – that will indicate that it is cooked.

T55 flour is available in some supermarkets; otherwise, find it online. I have also used strong bread flour with good results if you are unable to get T55.

Roast Carrot & Sunflower Seed Bread

Roast Carrot & Sunflower Seed Bread

Makes 8 rolls | Prep time 3 hours | Cook time 20 minutes

Ingredients

200g carrots, peeled and roughly chopped
1 clove garlic, finely chopped
1 teaspoon chilli flakes
1 teaspoon dried mixed herbs
2 teaspoons sea salt
Black pepper
2 tablespoons olive oil
400g strong white flour
10g dried active yeast
340ml lukewarm water
100g pumpkin seeds

Method

• Preheat the oven to 200°C/400°F/Gas 4.

• Put the carrots, garlic, chilli flakes, herbs, salt and pepper into a large baking tray, pour over the oil and mix to coat the carrots well. Cook in the oven for about 30 minutes until the carrots are soft and starting to caramelise.

• Put the contents of the baking tray into a food processor and pulse until everything is in very small chunks but not puréed.

• In a large mixing bowl, combine the flour, yeast, water and pumpkin seeds with the carrots until a dough has formed.

• Tip the dough onto a well-floured work surface and knead for 5-10 minutes. Put the dough into a lightly oiled bowl, cover with a tea towel and leave

Roasting carrots adds another dimension to their flavour that works so well in these rolls.

to rise for approximately 2 hours, or until doubled in size.

- Preheat the oven to 240°C/475°F/Gas 9.

- Tip onto a lightly floured surface, cut the dough into 8 equal pieces and shape each piece into a roll.

- Put the rolls on a non-stick baking sheet (you'll probably need 2).

- Leave in a warm place until well risen, about 20 minutes. Bake in the oven for 15-20 minutes until golden and the underside sounds hollow when tapped.

- Cool on a cooling rack.

Focaccia

This is a great bread to tear and share either al fresco in the summer sunshine or with a bowl of hearty soup by the fireside in winter.

Focaccia

Serves 6-8 | Prep time 2¾ hours | Cook time 30 minutes

Ingredients

For the dough:
500g strong white flour
7g salt
10g dried active yeast
2 tablespoons olive oil
350ml lukewarm water

For the topping:
2 medium red onions, chopped
1 tablespoon olive oil
10-12 olives, halved
6-8 cherry tomatoes, halved
2-3 sprigs fresh rosemary
Sea salt

Method

• Mix the flour, salt and yeast in a large mixing bowl. Make a well in the centre and pour in the olive oil and water.

• Bring all the ingredients together with your hand to form a dough.

• Tip the dough out onto a lightly floured surface and knead for 5-10 minutes until you have a soft, elastic dough.

• Put the dough into a lightly oiled mixing bowl, cover and leave to rise for about 2 hours or until doubled in size.

• In the meantime, sweat the onions in the olive oil on a low heat for around 10 minutes. Set aside, reserving the oil also.

- When the dough has risen, turn it out onto a lightly floured surface and knead lightly for 30 seconds. Stretch and shape the dough to fit a lightly oiled baking tray (about 26 x 34cm). Cover and leave to rise for 20-30 minutes.

- Preheat the oven to 220°C/425°F/Gas 7.

- When the dough is well risen, make several indentations with your fingers and put the olives and tomatoes into the holes.

- Scatter the dough with the red onions and the oil from the pan. Remove the rosemary leaves from the sprigs and scatter on, along with some sea salt.

- Bake for about 30 minutes until the bread is golden brown and the onions have caramalised. Turn out onto a nice wooden board, tear into chunks and eat warm or cold.

Curry Stuffed Bread Rolls

Makes 8 rolls | Prep time 2 ¾ hours | Cook time 20 minutes

Ingredients

For the dough:

500g strong white bread flour

14g dried active yeast

10g salt

330ml water

2 tablespoons olive oil

For the filling:

1 tablespoon rapeseed or olive oil

2 medium onions, diced

4-5 medium-sized potatoes, peeled and diced into 1cm pieces

2 teaspoons panch phoron

3 cloves garlic, peeled and finely chopped

4 fresh green chillies, finely sliced

1 teaspoon ground cumin

1 teaspoon ground coriander

1 teaspoon ground amchaar powder

1 teaspoon ground turmeric

Pinch dried curry leaves

Small handful golden sultanas

1 teaspoon garam masala

Salt

Method

- Mix the flour, yeast and salt together in a large bowl. Pour in the water and oil and bring together to form a dough. Tip out onto a floured surface and knead for 10 minutes until the dough is smooth and elastic. Put the dough into a clean, lightly oiled bowl, cover and leave to rise for about 2 hours, or until doubled in size.

- In the meantime, heat the oil in a large heavy-based frying pan, add the onions, potatoes and panch phoron and cook for about 5 minutes, stirring from time to time, before adding the garlic, chillies, all the spices and the sultanas. Add just enough water to cover the bottom of the pan. Cover and cook over gentle heat, stirring occasionally and adding a little more water as the potatoes absorb it.

- Once the potatoes are tender, remove from the heat, set aside and allow to cool.

I created these when all my family were taking lunch boxes to work and were getting a bit fed up of the ubiquitous sandwiches! They would also be great for picnics, or with soup for a wholesome lunch. Serve hot or cold.

- Preheat the oven to 230°C/450°F/Gas 8.

- When the dough has risen, tip it onto a lightly floured surface and divide into 8 equal pieces. Knead each ball and then roll out with a rolling pin to circles (about 5" diameter). Put a heaped tablespoon of the potato mixture into each circle of dough. Brush the edges with a little water and fold to encase the filling. Place the rolls fold-side down on a lightly floured baking tray. You'll need 2 trays.

- Leave the rolls in a warm place to rise for 20-25 minutes, covered with a clean tea towel.

- Bake for 15-20 minutes until golden brown.

Sauces &
Chutneys

Fat Hen Pesto

Prep time 10 minutes | Cook time 0 minutes

Ingredients

100g young fat hen leaves, removed from their stalks, washed and patted dry

50g pine nuts

100ml olive oil (approximately)

Sea salt and black pepper

Method

- In a food processor, blend the fat hen and the pine nuts until coarsely chopped.

- Add the olive oil a bit at a time until you reach the pesto consistency that you like. Season well with the sea salt and black pepper.

This is a fantastic vibrant green colour. Stir it through pasta, drizzle onto tenderstem broccoli, broad beans or roast carrots, top pizza or swirl through houmous. The possibilities are endless!

Elderberry Vinegar

Prep time 5 days | Cook time 15 minutes

Ingredients

Elderberries
Sugar
White wine vinegar

Method

- Remove the elderberries from their umbels using a fork, or freeze the berries – whilst still frozen they are easy to remove from the stalks.

- Weigh the berries before placing them in a kilner jar or tub. Add 500ml of white wine vinegar for every 350g fruit.

- Leave covered for 3-5 days. Stir occasionally.

- Strain off the liquid and discard the berries. Add 350g of sugar per 250ml liquid.

- Simmer for 10-15 minutes then bottle.

Reuse and recycle old jars of all shapes and sizes to avoid waste.

Aubergine & Apple Chutney

Prep time 30 minutes | Cook time 1 hour

Ingredients

1kg aubergines
1 tablespoon salt
2 tablespoons cooking oil
500g cooking apples, peeled and grated
3 onions, diced
3-4 cloves garlic, very finely sliced
2-3 red chillies, finely chopped
1 thumb-sized piece of ginger, finely diced
1 (568ml) bottle of malt vinegar
450g unrefined golden granulated sugar
4 teaspoons panch phoron

2 teaspoons ground cumin
25g fresh coriander, chopped
2 bay leaves

The chutney can be eaten straight away, but it's probably best left to mature for a few weeks. It will keep unopened for several months or more.

I love making chutney, and they are a great way to use up a glut of homegrown produce.

Method

- Cut the aubergines into 5mm thick slices, sprinkle with salt, place into a colander and leave to stand for about an hour.

- Rinse off the aubergines in water and pat dry with a tea towel. Cut the slices into smallish dice.

- Place the apples, onions, garlic, chillies, ginger, vinegar, sugar and spices into a large pan and bring to the boil.

- Heat the oil in a large frying pan. When very hot, add the aubergine in 2-3 batches. Fry the aubergine until it takes on a little colour then add to the rest of the chutney ingredients. Reduce the heat to a gentle simmer for about 1 hour or until all the ingredients are soft and the mixture has thickened.

- Remove from the heat, remove the bay leaves and carefully pour the chutney into sterilised jars. Cover and seal.

Spicy Carrot Chutney

Prep time 15 minutes | Cook time 1½ hours

Ingredients

1kg carrots, peeled and grated

2 medium onions, finely diced

2 large cloves garlic, peeled and finely chopped

Thumb-sized piece of ginger, finely chopped

½ scotch bonnet chilli, finely chopped

350g soft dark brown sugar

600ml vinegar

½ teaspoon red chilli flakes

2 teaspoons turmeric powder

2 teaspoons ground cumin

1½ teaspoons fenugreek seeds

1 teaspoon black onion seeds

10 dried curry leaves (approximately)

Sea salt and black pepper

1 handful of fresh coriander, chopped

Serve this chutney with burgers, in sandwiches, or on toast. Stir a little into houmous for a dip, or use it as an accompaniment to a curry.

Method

- Put the carrots, onions, garlic, ginger, scotch bonnet, sugar and vinegar into a large saucepan on medium heat. Mix together for about 5 minutes, stirring regularly, until all the sugar has dissolved.

- Add the spices, salt and pepper and bring to the boil. Reduce the heat to a simmer and continue to cook for about 1¼ hours.

- Add the chopped coriander and stir through.

- Drag a large spoon through the mixture – if no liquid fills the channel you have made, then the chutney is ready. If it is still a bit wet, simply continue to cook gently until the right consistency is achieved.

- Spoon the chutney into sterilised jars, cover and leave to cool. Leave to mature for 1-2 weeks before opening. The chutney will keep unopened for several months or more.

Metric and imperial equivalents

Weights	Solid	Volume	Liquid
15g	½oz	15ml	½ floz
25g	1oz	30ml	1 floz
40g	1½oz	50ml	2 floz
50g	1¾oz	100ml	3½ floz
75g	2¾oz	125ml	4 floz
100g	3½oz	150ml	5 floz (¼ pint)
125g	4½oz	200ml	7 floz
150g	5½oz	250ml	9 floz
175g	6oz	300ml	10 floz (½ pint)
200g	7oz	400ml	14 floz
250g	9oz	450ml	16 floz
300g	10½oz	500ml	18 floz
400g	14oz	600ml	1 pint (20 floz)
500g	1lb 2oz	1 litre	1¾ pints
1kg	2lb 4oz	1.2 litre	2 pints
1.5kg	3lb 5oz	1.5 litre	2¾ pints
2kg	4lb 8oz	2 litres	3½ pints
3kg	6lb 8oz	3 litres	5¼ pints